STRONG IN THE TIME OF TESTING

STRONG IN THE TIME OF TESTING

M. BASILEA SCHLINK

KANAAN PUBLICATIONS
Evangelical Sisterhood of Mary
Darmstadt, Germany and Radlett, England

Original title: *Jesus, Du machst mich stark*
First German edition 1993

First British edition 1993
published by Kanaan Publications

ISBN 1 897647 03 4

Compiled mainly from excerpts from *The Eve of Persecution* and *Prayers in preparation for the near future* by the same author. (Original titles *Kurz vor der Christenverfolgung—Liebe will leiden*, 1974, and *Notzeitgebete für die nahe Zukunft*, 1979.)

Designed and Produced in England by
Nuprint Ltd, Station Road, Harpenden, Herts AL5 4SE.

Contents

Prayers

Dear Brothers and Sisters in Christ,

There is a heavy burden on my heart. Persecution of Christians is arising worldwide after penetrating more and more countries in the last few decades. When in the early nineteen-nineties oppression was lifted in some countries where persecution had been severe, this was truly a miracle of God. However, there is no saying how long this respite will last. The forces hostile to Christianity could swiftly become active again. We cannot afford to ignore the basic trend of our world, which has turned its back on God.

Christians in the West are now facing growing pressures and sometimes outright persecution. For all of us who love the Lord the time is coming when we will be called upon to suffer or even lay down our lives for Him who is so blasphemed and degraded today. I feel deep anguish at the thought of the physical, mental and spiritual pain awaiting those who remain faithful to Him.

Who will be able to endure such distress?—Only those who have prepared themselves. They will have the strength to overcome and be loyal to Jesus in great affliction. Those who practise now by making a stand for the Lord, by willingly bearing every hardship in their lives and by trusting in the Father's faithfulness, will have the strength to endure. Those who keep their eyes on Jesus and pray for an ardent love for Him will receive grace to suffer.

If we prepare ourselves today, we will have the courage to face tomorrow and be able to suffer for Jesus' sake. Then He will be glorified. If this is our earnest plea, He will grant it, since He has promised to answer prayer.

Yours in Jesus' love,
Mother Basilea

The Lamb of God so silently
Now makes His way to Calvary,
His little lambs behind Him.
Each bears his cross in love for Him
Who goes ahead, the Paschal Lamb,
And bids them, 'Oh, stay by Me!'

He looks upon them lovingly,
His faithful ones encouraging
To go on without tiring,
Shows them the wounds that brought Him death,
From which His precious blood flows forth,
Giving them grace to suffer.

In loving union with their Lord,
His followers press on heavenward,
Each one his cross embracing.
And from their gently bleeding wounds
Blessings flow forth to others too.
How blest to follow Jesus!

Chapter 1

Trusting God for Today and Tomorrow

For a little while you may have to suffer various trials, so that the genuineness of your faith, more precious than gold which though perishable is tested by fire, may redound to praise and glory and honour at the revelation of Jesus Christ.

1 Peter 1:6–7

LET US BE REALISTIC. Will any of us be able to endure persecution?—Not if we rely on our own strength and resources. However, we can meet the future triumphantly if we count on the omnipotence of God, our heavenly Father. This factor will tip the balance in our favour. He possesses all the strength we lack and will demonstrate His power when we undergo persecution.

This calls for a complete change in our way of thinking. We must discard any idea of self-reliance, since from the very outset it is obvious that our powers of endurance will not be adequate in suffering. But our heavenly Father will stand by us, demonstrating His might and lending us aid in times of testing. Everything hinges on whether or not we reckon with Him. His power is so immense that our ability to suffer grows insignificant by comparison. It makes no difference how great our powers of endurance are or whether we have none at all. To God it is the same whether He has to impart much or little of His strength to us. Indeed, the weak have the Lord's special promise: 'My power is made perfect in weakness' (2 Corinthians 12:9).

The way we react to our daily trials is decisive. When we can no longer see a way out of our predicament, we need to reckon alone with God and His assistance, for He has given us a definite pledge of help and He is what His name says: Yes and Amen. Because He is faithful to His promises, we will experience now, and later during persecution, the truth of His words: 'I will never fail you nor forsake you' (Hebrews 13:5); 'Fear not, for I am with you... I will strengthen you, I will help you, I will uphold you with my victorious right hand' (Isaiah 41:10). We only have to do our part by claiming in faith the promise, coming to God our Father in every sorrow and saying to Him,

> Abba, dearest Father, I trust You.
> You will uphold me and carry me through.
> You are with me.
> You will bring me the help I need.
> I take refuge in Your heart.
> When I am united with You, nothing can harm me.
> You are my shield, and Your angels watch over me.

If we approach God in deep trust, we will experience His aid, provided we come as true children of His with humble and contrite hearts. This means lying at the foot of the cross, confessing our sins to God and before others, and receiving forgiveness through Jesus' blood every time we have failed. Grace is promised to penitent sinners. God draws near to the humble and helps them, whereas He opposes the proud and self-righteous. It is very important that we approach affliction and persecution in a spirit of humility and repentance. Then God will stand by us and grant us His fatherly help.

In times of persecution the Father Himself will carry us through. We do not need to rely on ourselves, for He has pledged Himself to intervene on our behalf. Some of the happenings will seem so miraculous that they could have come straight from the pages of the Bible. A twentieth-century report from White Russia tells how night after night, in an unheated cell, a girl was made to sleep on the cold cement floor. It was winter-time and she had no outer garment to keep her warm. Yet she testified, 'Every night when I lay down in that icy grave, I committed myself into the hands of God and—it was a miracle!—a warm current of air surrounded me all night long and I could rest well.' This was obviously God's doing. He is able to lessen or cancel even the pain and effects of torture.

Riotous gangs and terrorists may threaten us, but they can do nothing to us without God's permission. If, after many instances of protection and deliverance, the time should come for some of us to lay down our lives for Jesus, we may experience other miracles of God, like Stephen, the first Christian martyr (Acts 6–7). Stephen was given a glimpse into the open heavens. He did not despair in the face of a cruel death by stoning. On the contrary, he was filled with divine joy and was even capable of forgiving his torturers.

There is a moving testimony from China. An elder of a small church was taken to court because of his faith in Christ. After a savage beating, he was thrown into prison, only to be released a few days later without any explanation. At the next worship service, he gave his testimony to the assembled church, which had been praying for him without ceasing during his imprisonment. 'When I received the 240 lashes, I thought of Stephen and how he was stoned. Then I had an experience similar to his. Above me I saw Jesus, for whom I was suffering, and I was comforted beyond words. It was as though a hand were laid upon my mangled back so that I no longer felt the pain. Also, the Lord told me that I would be set free in a few days, and that really did happen, as you can all see.' His eyes still shone with the Lord's comfort. He had about him the dignity and glory distinguishing those who have suffered disgrace for Jesus' sake.

Once long ago God uttered a command and out of nothing He made heaven and earth, a marvellous creation. The same God who lives today needs say but a word and that which would normally cause us agony or injury will be rendered ineffective. He intervenes and grants us help when we appeal to Him in our need. God the Father, who does not forget the young ravens that cry, does not forget any of His children when they call upon Him. His attention is especially drawn to those who are suffering for love of Him and are in fear and distress. He cannot forget them or leave them without comfort and help. That would be to contradict His very nature. And God cannot deny Himself. Our loving heavenly Father is also the Almighty, who has promised to show us His love and to exercise His omnipotence on our behalf.

In darkest night, behold, a light
Enkindled midst the darkness,
A shining light, unfailing, bright.
It tells us, 'Trust in God's word.'

For times of grief, there is relief,
A gracious outcome waiting.
The Father cares, your pain He shares,
Brings light amid the darkness.

So persevere and do not fear:
God always keeps His promise.
Oh, raise the song, 'His help will come,
For God has planned my pathway.'

One of the watchwords for this preparatory time when we are faced with problems and suffering is, 'Pray! Run to the Father!' God is waiting for His child to come so that He can help him. Let us beg the Father for help and take refuge in His strong arms, which will carry us through. If we practise doing so now, we will also turn to Him in time of persecution. When too exhausted and pain-ridden to formulate long prayers, we only have to say, 'My Father, I trust You!' Let us say this over and over again. It is a powerful prayer and will bring us help, for we receive according to our trust. Either God will save us from our plight or we will experience His loving presence so wonderfully that the horrors about us will fade away.

As our Father in Jesus Christ, God is worthy of our implicit trust. He has not only expressed His love in words; He has demonstrated it. Although we have burdened and wearied Him with our sins, grieved Him and so often rebelled against Him, He sacrificed

His beloved Son for us with an aching heart. The Father's love and faithfulness have been tried and proven; they are absolutely reliable. His love does not change; His heart is the same today.

Long ago God made the supreme sacrifice of His only Son, as proof of His love, in order to save us and open heaven for us. Will He not lavish His love upon those who are no longer His enemies but His children, who have come to love Him as their Father? This He will do especially when they are undergoing suffering and persecution for Jesus' sake. He will pour out His heart of love upon them in their grief and pain, turning hell into heaven.

O Father, dearest Father,
Within Your hands I rest.
Lord, You can transform all things;
All power You possess.

I rest in You, safe hidden,
O dearest Father mine.
When fears and cares surround me,
In You deep peace I find.

Within Your heart I'm resting;
Your love enfolds me there.
Your heart knows all my suffering
And how much I can bear.

My heart in fear and sorrow
May rest in quietness.
I trust in Your will wholly
And this is blessedness.

Chapter 2

Knit to His Will, We Are Strong

Going a little farther he fell on his face and prayed, 'My Father, if it be possible, let this cup pass from me; nevertheless, not as I will, but as thou wilt.' Matthew 26:39

WHEN THE ENEMIES of Jesus came to take Him prisoner in the Garden of Gethsemane, He met them with the words, 'I am He!' Jesus was prepared to suffer, to be imprisoned, to be tried and scourged, since His will was one with the Father's. We, too, may have to face arrest. But being one with the will of God means being united with God Himself, and this makes us strong in the hour of deepest affliction. Being united with God means we have entered a covenant with the almighty, immortal God, who contends for us. Being united with Jesus Christ means having at our side the risen, victorious Lord, to whom all powers and principalities are subject. When we are united with the Almighty, we will be able to master every situation. This union with God is essential for the time of persecution, but it has to be practised now, for unity with God, which means unity with His will, does not come to us easily.

So often our will clashes with God's. His leadings oppose our natural inclinations. We find it hard to accept His will, for instance, when it means submitting to those who insult us or act against our personal wishes and opinions. How quick we are to protest and rebel, thus defying the will of God! Because our unity with God is broken, our strength to overcome in suffering is also broken. When our will revolts against God's will, a barrier is erected between God and us, and we have to undergo the painful experience of having God against us, for 'God opposes the proud' (1 Peter 5:5), who set their wills against His.

During persecution we will have to suffer the consequences for each time we defied God's will and leadings by asserting our own wishes and will instead: we will be weak. The reverse is equally true. Every acceptance of God's will now in our daily trials and personal sorrows will be rewarded. The repeated dedication of our will binds us more and more tightly to God, forming a union that will hold in the mental and physical pain of persecution. When we are united with God, nothing can harm us.

The prayer 'Yes, Father!' should become like second nature to us by the time persecution breaks out. We need to practise now, so that every time our hearts say No to God's leadings, this No will be turned into a Yes. It is vital that we declare war on the spirit of defiance that arises in us when our will is thwarted, remembering that others can do nothing to us without God's permission. By the time persecution comes, may our will be completely knit to His will through repeated commitments to suffering.

Are we capable of surrendering our will unconditionally to the will of God? Are we capable of saying 'Yes, Father!', even when it demands our life, our all? We will be if we bear the true image of God in our hearts and declare who God is. God is love; His will is goodness; His thoughts, purposes and decisions come from a fatherly heart brimming over with love. He has only the best intentions for us, His children, even though we may not understand His actions.

My life in every detail
Was planned by God in love.
A heart of purest goodness
Is guiding from above.

And though the way before me
Lies hidden from my eyes,
How deeply reassuring
To know God's plans are wise:

With everlasting wisdom
Each single step conceived!
So I will fear not suffering:
God wants the best for me.

And when I fail to fathom
The purpose of my trials,
I trust God's loving wisdom
In caring for His child.

A glimpse of the Father's heart will move us to repeat the prayer, 'Yes, Father!', no matter how hard we find His leadings; and in time this prayer will knit us to the will of God completely. This loving union is essential. Otherwise we will not be able to stand our ground during the persecution ahead. A half-hearted commitment to His will—sometimes submitting but at other times resisting when our will is thwarted in a particular situation—is not enough.

It will not hold. A wall made of loose bricks will collapse on the impact of a storm. In order to withstand the storm, the bricks must be cemented together.

The same principle applies to our lives. If we take advantage of the countless opportunities today for making great or small commitments of the will, our union with God will become firm and unshakeable. Then during affliction we will be united with our loving Father in His omnipotence and with Jesus Christ, who is Lord of all. As Lord and God, Jesus has only to speak a word and a prison door will swing open, a trial will take a direction in our favour, and medications and drugs intended to weaken our resistance and make us pliable will be ineffective (see Mark 16:18). And at cross-examinations the Holy Spirit, the Spirit of wisdom, will help us, inspiring us with the right words. Indeed, when we are knit to the will of God, we are invincible, for His will is stronger than any other will.

In the midst of persecution we will rest in the Father's arms like a child. The evil and suffering others plan to inflict upon us cannot harm us. United with God, we are strong and capable of enduring just like the martyrs in past centuries. Reports from various countries testify of the supernatural strength bestowed on Christians suffering for their faith. 'I feel better than ever! The joy of the Lord is our strength,' wrote a young believer after her second term in a labour camp. This joy came from committing herself to the will of God.

If we are united with Christ, it does not matter what trouble or danger befalls us. 'Who shall separate us from the love of Christ? Shall tribulation, or distress, or persecution, or famine, or nakedness, or peril, or sword?' (Romans 8:35). None of these, for He has promised to remain in us if we remain in Him (John 15:4).

In deepest throes of pain and woe
You're not alone if you but hope
In God, your Lord.

He cares for you, so rest assured.
In love He sends the very best
For you, His child.

He saved your soul, so be consoled.
He knows the way, His hand He lays
Upon His child.

Believe He's there; do not despair,
For when He seems beyond your reach,
He's very near.

Chapter 3

❧

The Right Perspective

...Looking to Jesus the pioneer and perfecter of our faith.
Hebrews 12:2

WHEN BOMBARDED BY the media with scenes of suffering, are we gripped with a sense of foreboding? The sight of people afflicted in body, soul and spirit, exiled and harassed, accentuates the reality of persecution awaiting Christians. We can envisage what it will be like when commandos break into houses, dragging away the Christians and torturing them. The mere thought of such horrors is petrifying. This is precisely what Satan hopes to achieve, for he is behind the persecution and terrorization of Christians. A person crippled with fear is incapable of fighting the good fight, and there is no victory without a battle—no way of triumphing amid suffering and torment for Jesus' sake.

We need to be strong for the time of persecution and, indeed, we will be invincible if we have the right perspective. We are influenced by what we look at. Therefore it is imperative that our minds are not filled with scenes of diabolic hatred and violence. If we dwell upon the coming horrors, picturing them in detail, we are lost. Fear will overcome us and drag us down into the slough of despair. We must turn our eyes away altogether and set our gaze on Jesus Christ, the Prince of Victory. He has destroyed the works of hell and continues to overthrow strongholds of the evil one. Victorious might emanates from Jesus, imparting strength to us and helping us to stand firm. Looking to Him in faith is our only resort now, and later when we are in peril.

When we turn our eyes upon Jesus, comfort is poured into our fearful hearts. This we will experience during persecution and at the mere prospect of it. One glance at our Saviour and Helper transforms us and our situation. In particular, the sight of our Lord humiliated and crowned with thorns implants in our souls the willingness to suffer. His infinite love is revealed to us in His suffering. But if the sufferings of Jesus do not have a place in our lives, we cannot suffer for Him. Today more than ever let us take time to contemplate His sufferings; then we will come very close to Him and our own suffering will seem small.

Unto You alone, my Saviour,
I would look when I must suffer,
And behold Your countenance.
Gazing on Your noble features,
My heart drinks its fill, O Jesus,
And all horrors fade away.

To behold You, Lord, derided,
Crowned with thorns and so tormented,
Gives me strength to suffer too.
When in love You look upon me,
Darkness and despair flee from me
And Your comfort fills my soul.

Jesus appeals to us to look at Him when dread threatens to overwhelm us; then the darkness which is gathering about us and even seeking to enter our innermost being will be turned into light. His countenance is like the radiant sun, sending forth rays of light and dispelling all gloom in our hearts.

We have to confront the future. Indeed, Jesus challenges us to realize the significance of the present age and to read the signs of the times (Matthew 16:3). He wants us to take advantage of the time left before persecution breaks out and to prepare ourselves.

Strength flows into us as we rest our eyes upon Jesus' countenance. His countenance illumines the whole universe and shines upon those in deep distress and affliction, ministering comfort. If we look to Jesus, becoming completely absorbed in Him, we will be filled with peace and gripped with a joy that is not of this world.

O countenance of my Redeemer,
You shine like the sun in its splendour,
O loveliest countenance, noble, divine,
Aglow with God's majesty, holy, sublime.

O countenance, so awe-inspiring,
I kneel down in reverence, adoring.
Oh, help me to keep my eyes fixed upon You.
The things of this world disappear as the dew.

All misery fades into nothing
For Jesus' disciples beholding
His countenance radiant with glory and love,
Reflecting the strength of the Father above.

The right perspective will save us during persecution. But this is something that needs to be acquired now, and time is short. The way we approach our everyday trials casts the die for later. It is vital that we see beyond these problems, not allowing them to absorb, cripple and oppress us. We need to turn our eyes instead upon Jesus, through whom heaven and earth were made. He looks upon us lovingly, promising to help.

In the hour of darkness He will reveal Himself even more, letting His infinite love, glory and power shine upon us in our night. This we can count on. As we fasten our eyes on His countenance, we will drink in the love He radiates and receive His help. Rapt in His gaze, we will no longer be haunted by the faces of our torturers or engrossed by the horrors and appalling conditions. Jesus alone, our Lord and King, will fill our hearts as we experience the power that comes from beholding Him, our suffering and victorious Lord.

In His love Jesus looks at us, waiting for us to return His gaze and to keep our eyes fixed upon Him during times of anguish and distress. His name is a great source of power and He waits for us to pronounce it as we behold Him: 'Jesus, my Helper. Jesus, my Saviour. Jesus, my Bridegroom.' In our present sorrows and troubles we must learn to look to Him and call upon His name. We need to escape from the vicious circle of revolving round ourselves and our problems and to contemplate His sufferings instead. Then our suffering will grow insignificant. We can trust in His power and His promises of love and help. As we look to Him, calling upon His victorious name, we will be delivered from the slough of despair. Our souls will be restored and we will have the comforting assurance of His presence.

> Someone stands beside me, I am not alone;
> Someone shares my suffering and sorrow unknown—
> Jesus, my Helper and Victor.

Chapter 4

Victory Over Sin

Your adversary the devil prowls around like a roaring lion, seeking some one to devour. Resist him, firm in your faith.
1 Peter 5:8–9

DURING THIS SHORT TIME on earth everything depends on our overcoming in the hour of trial awaiting us as Christians. Will we stand the test of suffering and persecution? Will our faith prove itself in the furnace of affliction? The outcome will decide our eternal destiny. During persecution Satan will try to get at us through the pain inflicted by demonized people. He intends to defeat us and rob us of our heavenly crown. Satan's strategy will be to attack us where we are most vulnerable. He will take advantage, for instance, of our fear of suffering, cowardice, rebellion, false emotional attachments, or fear of displeasing others.

When persecution breaks out, it will become evident how seriously we took sin in our lives and to what extent we fought and overcame it. We will not be spared the consequences if we have been so taken up with trivial and mundane affairs, the sorrows and joys of *today,* that we have forgotten *tomorrow.* Tomorrow will bring persecution. No one can stand this test unless he has prepared himself in advance by fighting an earnest battle against sin through faith in Jesus' redemption.

The Bible instructs us to lay aside sin, which clings to us and weighs us down (Hebrews 12:1). Why? Sin weakens us. Normally, if we are bound to others, dependent on their praise and love, overanxious to please, or afraid of giving offence, we will not be able to stand our ground during cross-examinations. Bondage to people and to the things of this world ultimately binds us to Satan, bringing us under his influence. And as a result we weaken and succumb and even become capable of denying Jesus, thus forfeiting our eternal heritage in glory.

It is written of the persecuted Christians in the last times: 'They have conquered him [Satan] by the blood of the Lamb...' (Revelation 12:11). But when do we use the word 'conquer'?—Only when a battle is involved, for there is no victory without a battle. And when are we willing to fight the battle of faith so as to be freed from our slavery to sin?—Only when we refuse to tolerate our sins, such as quarrelsomeness, the desire to dominate, envy, self-will, untruthfulness, the gratification of our drives, and really hate them. Not until we realize that such sinning is a grievous offence against God and man, do we seek release at any price. Then we are willing to fight against our sins to the utmost and with a view to being prepared for the future.

The crucial question for the time of persecution is: Will sin still be able to weaken me then to the extent it does now, or will I be victorious, having fought against my sin beforehand? Only if we have let the blood of Jesus release us beforehand from our bondage to food and sleep, ease and comfort, will we be strong enough to endure hunger, thirst and physical suffering. Only if we have overcome bitterness, unwillingness to forgive and rebellion now in our everyday lives, will we be able to bear our betrayers and torturers in patience and love, and to forgive them. Thus equipped, we will not be defeated by Satan in the hour of testing.

Now is the time to prepare. Jesus' admonition to build our house upon rock and not upon sand, so that it will stand in the impending storm, is highly relevant (Matthew 7:21–27). When the floods come, only that which has a firm foundation—that is, a life of discipleship rather than our knowledge of Christian truths—will not be swept away. Doing the will of God, rather than saying, 'Lord, Lord', is what counts, according to Jesus. And what is the will of God?—Our sanctification (1 Thessalonians 4:3). This does not imply sinlessness, for we are sinners till our dying breath. Sanctification is a life-long process including the battle of faith against sin, so that we may be transformed into Jesus' likeness.

In this battle of faith we need to take the right measures. 'If your right eye causes you to sin, pluck it out and throw it away' (Matthew 5:29). This means taking action. I need to confess my sins to God and also to others by admitting where I have failed and humbly asking their forgiveness for sinning against them time and again. How decisive are the words, 'Please forgive me; I am very sorry'!

Do we yield to our sinful inclinations? Have we formed false attachments to others? Are we bound to our hobbies or to money? Are we addicted to stimulants or tranquillizers? Are we on bad terms with someone? Are we envious? Or are we so egoistic that we cannot bear to be disturbed? Then there should be a U-turn in our lives. We should give God an indication that our desire to become free is in earnest, though only Jesus can actually bring us release from enslavement to sin. And we will discover, 'If the Son makes you free, you will be free indeed' (John 8:36).

Every time we look to Jesus in faith, every time we pray to Him in faith, our fetters are loosened further; but we also have to humble ourselves beneath His hand, submitting patiently to His chastening and trusting in His victory until we experience release. A persevering faith will turn us into overcomers, enabling us to stand firm even under the pressure of persecution.

In particular, we need to tackle cowardice and a man-pleasing attitude. Otherwise, for fear of displeasing others, we may be disloyal to our convictions. During persecution it is essential that we are capable of bearing witness to Jesus. Only if we are willing to stand up and be counted for Jesus now, will we be able to do so later when it costs us far more. Today, when God Himself is being attacked and blasphemy has reached unheard-of proportions, the challenge to make a stand for the Lord is urgent. Jesus is being subjected to the most outrageous indignities, mockery and degradation. By attributing all sorts of obscenities to Him, people try to sanction their own perverse lifestyles. Numerous films, stage productions and publications reveal how far man dares to go in blaspheming the holy Son of God.

Are we making a stand for Jesus? Do we voice our disapproval when He is treated this way? This is what we are being asked today. It takes courage to be a true witness. To be ridiculed as 'old-fashioned' or 'pharisaical' is humiliating, but we should never remain silent or conform to the crowd for the sake of being thought relevant, understanding, broad-minded, sophisticated or modern.

This battle against a false sense of brotherly love, false emotional ties and dependence upon the opinions and approval of others becomes increasingly vital as persecution spreads throughout the world. The day is coming when we, too, may be called upon to lay down our lives for the Lord as the supreme proof of our loyalty.

We cannot be alert enough in view of the satanic attempts to lull us to sleep and to cloud our thinking. We need to resist these attacks and fight the battle against sin, especially cowardice, the tendency to go with the crowd, and a false tolerance. Then God will do everything to help us be steadfast during persecution, so that we may be counted worthy of joining the overcomers in heaven who 'have conquered him [Satan]...by the word of their testimony, for they loved not their lives even unto death' (Revelation 12:11).

Chapter 5

The Privilege of Suffering for Christ

It has been granted to you that for the sake of Christ you should not only believe in him but also suffer for his sake.
Philippians 1:29

PERSECUTION OF CHRISTIANS looms ahead on a scale probably never seen before—a fact which is enough to make anyone afraid. Brainwashing, labour camps, prisons, psychiatric clinics, torture, martyrdom come to mind. Yet there is something special about this suffering, for it is quite different from other afflictions. It is suffering *for Christ*.

We are not suffering for some concept, nor for a sinful, mortal man idolized by the masses. We are not suffering for the sake of a ruler who deludes his people, perhaps even terrorizing them. Thousands commit themselves to such leaders, not stopping at any sacrifice and prepared even to die for them, only to discover that they had been deceived. How often this has happened in the past!

As Christians, however, we have the wonderful privilege of suffering and risking our lives for Jesus Christ during persecution. He is the Lord Most High, exalted and reigning in majesty. As the Son of God radiating glory, love, righteousness and truth, He is unique. The greatest man on earth cannot begin to compare with Him. He is altogether different, without sin. He is the Mighty God, through whom the world was made (Hebrews 1:2). Yet in His amazing love for us, He became the Man of Sorrows, despised and rejected by all, suffering an agonizing death for our sakes. Again today, as the humble, meek Lamb of God, He patiently endures blasphemy, degradation and bitter shame. Today Jesus is calling us to His side more than ever before to suffer disgrace, contempt and persecution with Him. Let us give Him the response of our love, for He is worthy of it.

It is truly remarkable that sinners are privileged to suffer for Jesus. He is Lord of lords. On the cross He disarmed the powers and principalities, triumphing over them (Colossians 2:15), and one day He will display His victory over Satan before all the world.

To be God's co-workers labouring for the advance of His eternal kingdom (1 Corinthians 3:9) is incredible enough, considering that we are sinful, mortal beings. Yet it is utterly amazing that by our suffering, too, we are to be His co-workers and thus partners with Christ our Lord, who builds His kingdom through suffering. To suffer for Jesus and to help establish the Kingdom of God as 'a chosen instrument'—this was Paul's calling, as the Lord confirmed in His words, 'I will show him how much he must suffer for the sake of my name' (Acts 9:16).

Martyrs of the Early Christian era and of our times were conscious of the tremendous honour of not only believing in Jesus but suffering for Him. Paul considered it an act of grace, a privilege (Philippians 1:29). The martyrs were usually filled with a joy that was not of this world. Why?—Because their hearts were set on fire with love for Jesus. Thus they were overwhelmed at the honour of bearing shame and disgrace and many hardships for His name's sake. To them the name of Jesus represented all glory and might, wisdom and beauty, and immeasurable love. His name always sounded in their hearts as the sweetest name.

The martyrs of recent years, like those of the past, could only endure persecution and suffering for Jesus with joy and dedication because Jesus was their first and foremost love. Love compelled them, even before persecution had broken out, to share Jesus' life, which was marked by lowliness, humiliation, disappointments, privation, misunderstanding, insults, rejection, self-denial, sacrifice and, finally, the cross. Those who for love of Jesus had already chosen His pathway were practising true discipleship by the time persecution came. They were tried and tested in suffering and aflame with love for Him. The more they practised bearing their cross with Jesus, the closer they drew to Him and the more fiercely blazed the fire of their love.

Jesus loves us greatly and desires our love in return. He entreats us to love Him and to choose His pathway, taking up our cross and following Him.

Constrained by love and thanks, I long to be
Close by Your side, although my heart should grieve,
O suffering Lord.

I want to walk with You, Lord Jesus Christ.
And though Your path means pain and sacrifice,
I'll follow You.

Today there is still time to practise true discipleship of the cross, so that when persecution comes, we will be trained in suffering. Jesus appeals to us with greater urgency than ever before because so much is at stake. He challenges us to set foot on His pathway and bear suffering of the body and soul with dedication. If for love of Jesus we are willing to endure humiliations, disappointments and injustice, saying ever anew, 'For You, with You, Lord Jesus', our love will grow strong and we will become experienced in suffering.

This is a gradual process. The first stage in committing ourselves to suffering is to say, 'Lord Jesus, as Your disciple I am *called* to suffer for You!' By the second stage we are able to say, 'I am *ready* to suffer for You!' But by the third stage we can say, 'I am *privileged* to suffer for You; it is an honour to be counted worthy of this.' So let us make it our aim of faith to reach this third stage. Each new act of dedication will bring us closer to it. During persecution we will reap the fruits of this time of practice, and the bitterness of suffering will be turned into rejoicing: 'Now I can show Jesus my love by suffering for Him, after all that He suffered on my behalf.'

This triumphant joy and thanksgiving for the privilege of suffering for Jesus can be found in a letter from the Evangelical Christians/Baptists of the former Soviet Union, which they sent to all the churches in the world. At the Second Congress of their Council of Churches in 1970, these Baptists, the relatives of persecuted Christians, came together. Did they want to make an accusation? To complain of their suffering? To join in sorrowing for fellow Christians taken prisoner or to plead for their release? On the contrary, the letter reads, 'We have come together—fathers, mothers, sons and daughters of prisoners—to thank the Lord for our suffering for Christ.'

Suffering for Christ? Time and again—perhaps at night—we picture the terrors of persecution and violent revolutions. But when these fears threaten to oppress us, our hearts can suddenly be filled with light. One short phrase can effect total transformation: 'For Christ!' Fear of the future, of physical and mental suffering during persecution, is turned into comfort, peace and even triumphant joy when we look at Jesus, our Lord and Saviour, the Bridegroom of our souls. It is our privilege and desire to suffer for Jesus Christ, who is eternal joy, the glory of heaven and earth, the great love of those who belong to Him.

In view of the coming troubles let us cling to the Lord Jesus with all our hearts. Then we will become joyful in our present fears and later amid torment, for our hearts will be ringing with those blessed words, 'For You, Jesus, for You!' When, in 1919, the Baltic professor of theology Traugott Hahn was led off to be executed, the guards forced him to carry down the prison corridor a pail of human excrement. Seeing him so degraded, a fellow prisoner, Bishop Platon of the Orthodox Church, whispered to him, *'Radi Christa'* (for the sake of Christ).

These words contain a wonderful hidden power. When the presbyter Peter Wiens in the former Soviet Union was about to be deported to a labour camp, he said good-bye to his wife with the words *'Radi Christa'*, not knowing whether he would ever see her again. These words set his wife at peace and strengthened his son—as the latter testified—when he, too, was deported.

The true image of Jesus never shines so brightly as during persecution. At such times He manifests the greatness and power of His fervent love as He visits those suffering imprisonment for His sake. Cold, hell-like cells are transformed by Jesus' presence into a heavenly palace.

Even children suffering persecution discover the reality of the living Lord, who is at their side. They taste something of the hidden glory and the honour of being considered worthy to suffer for His name's sake. 'What is your suffering for Jesus?' a ten-year-old boy asked a Christian visiting a church in the former Soviet Union. This boy had been detained in a camp along with his brothers and sisters during the years when their parents were imprisoned. However, children and parents both left the camps with their faith deepened through suffering. Now the lad was eager to know whether a believer had already suffered for Jesus. Young though he was, he no doubt sensed that suffering for Jesus was an honour.

But not until eternity when we see the shining crowns on the heads of those who endured suffering, will we fully realize what a privilege it is to suffer for Jesus.

Who can measure the great treasure
Suffering and grief have brought?
Who has sight and understanding
For the good that pain has wrought?

Who may live there close to Jesus
In unending glory bright?

Those who shared the cross beside Him,
With the Lamb endured dark night.

'Blessed are you when men hate you, and when they exclude you and revile you, and cast out your name as evil, on account of the Son of man! Rejoice in that day, and leap for joy, for behold, your reward is great in heaven' (Luke 6:22–23). A wonderful reward lies in store—and soon, very soon, suffering will be turned into eternal glory and immeasurable joy.

What greater privilege could there be than to suffer for Jesus, who wants to recompense our suffering with a divine reward and eternal glory! Let us lift up our eyes to heaven, for one thought of heaven drives all suffering away.

Chapter 6

God's Eternal Plans

May those who sow in tears reap with shouts of joy! He that goes forth weeping, bearing the seed for sowing, shall come home with shouts of joy, bringing his sheaves with him.
Psalm 126:5–6

'I REJOICE IN MY SUFFERINGS for your sake,' the apostle Paul declares in Colossians 1:24. He realizes the privilege of completing in his flesh 'what is lacking in Christ's afflictions for the sake of his body, that is, the church'. Paul rejoices, knowing that his sufferings will have far-reaching effects. Through his tribulations he is privileged to have a part in God's eternal plans—an amazing thought! He is drawn into God's marvellous purposes for the Body of Christ.

What a tremendous commission for sinful human beings! Our sufferings for Jesus' sake are to contribute to something wonderful. This knowledge, this thought, will help us during persecution. We are not merely enduring the affliction that has been laid upon us, submitting to it and saying, 'Yes, Father!' Far more is involved. We are suffering for a definite purpose, for Christ and His Body. Jesus, the Lamb of God, gave His life as a sacrifice so that God's eternal plans for the Body of Christ, and later for the whole of creation and for all nations, could be fulfilled. Through our suffering we can have a part in these eternal purposes of God, helping to prepare the bride of the Lamb and so hasten the day of Jesus' return.

We are living in the last times, and the great day will come when God's plan for the bride of the Lamb will be fulfilled. Thus the persecution of Christians in the end times is highly significant, for the last measure of suffering must be added before the bride of the Lamb can be completed in number and attain maturity. The overcomers in heaven will be longing for this moment. On that day of immeasurable joy and glory a climax in God's saving purposes will be reached. What a privilege to help bring about this tremendous event by contributing our share in suffering! This prospect will make tribulation worthwhile for the present-day martyrs and give them the strength to be steadfast. For when the marriage feast of the Lamb begins, the kingdoms of this world will belong to the Lord.

What a privilege and high calling to suffer with Jesus! What an act of grace, what a special honour! Jesus, who at Calvary completed His sacrifice and thus redeemed the whole world, waits in humility for the members of His Body to suffer with Him and for Him. They have the privilege of contributing their share of suffering so that His eternal plans and purposes for mankind and the whole universe can be carried out. There is tremendous inherent power in suffering. It yields abundant fruit and results in victory, glory and resurrection.

Knowing this will give us the strength even to lay down our lives for Jesus. Suffering brings great blessing to others, for as the apostle Paul said, 'I endure everything for the sake of the elect, that they also may obtain the salvation which in Christ Jesus goes with eternal glory' (2 Timothy 2:10). During persecution we will have the privilege of suffering for our church or fellowship or for certain people, so that they may be saved, learn to overcome and reach full maturity in Christ.

'We believe that the Lord is gathering our tears and will pour them out upon the arid, seeking hearts of the Russian people,' said the Evangelical Christians/Baptists in the above-cited letter. Suffering and tears have power. In the time of persecution many tears will be shed, not only because of personal troubles. When we profess Jesus, we may endanger others, and often it is harder to see loved ones suffer than to suffer ourselves. Or sometimes those close to us may increase our griefs through their antagonism to Christianity. This can be most agonizing of all.

Yet the assurance remains: 'The Lord is gathering our tears and will pour them out.' Our tears will bring blessing to arid, seeking hearts. The grain of wheat falls into the ground during persecution, giving rise to new life and revival at other places. The martyrs are still the seeds of the Church.

It is truly amazing that we are to be taken into the fellowship of His sufferings (Philippians 3:10), which means suffering with Jesus for the sake of His Body, for His elect, for those who seek God, and for those who have fallen away from Him or are living in outright rebellion against Him. Our tears and affliction will help bring many to Jesus so that they can reach eternal glory. Suffering for Jesus, the King of kings, has far-reaching results.

The deeper and greater the ordeals, the more wonderful the fruit and glory. Accordingly, the sufferings of persecution, with its cross-examinations and torture, will bear immeasurable fruit. If Jesus rewards a cup of cold water offered in His name, then how much more will He reward suffering for His sake? Because He loves us so much, He shares our trials, looking upon us in deep gratitude for all that we endure for His sake. Uplifted by this hope, the apostles, who encountered great hardships and had to go through the fires of tribulation, so often struck a note of joy when writing of suffering. 'Rejoice in so far as you share Christ's sufferings, that you may also rejoice and be glad when his glory is revealed' (1 Peter 4:13).

It is eternity that counts. No words can express what awaits those who have suffered for Jesus in this life. In heaven they will see Him face to face and joy will flood their hearts. Unimagined happiness awaits them in eternity—jubilation, exultation and joyful laughter as a compensation for all the tears they have shed here.

Heaven is a reality. Heaven is what awaits us. The sorrows of this lifetime will come to an end, but there is no end to the glory that is prepared for us above. If we set our hearts and minds on the things above where Christ is (Colossians 3:1–2), we will be able to face persecution. Hope and expectation of the future joy will give us the strength to endure, and the crown of life will make affliction worthwhile.

In Revelation 20:4 the martyrs are promised that they will reign with Jesus, enthroned beside Him. What an amazing prospect! For all eternity to abide with Jesus, our first and foremost love, our Bridegroom and King! In the face of such glory, suffering must fade away. 'I consider that the sufferings of this present time are not worth comparing with the glory that is to be revealed to us' (Romans 8:18). These words of Scripture hold true for all suffering, but especially for persecution.

The glory of heaven will bring us incomprehensible joy and bliss for eternity, whereas the suffering of this life is limited. One day it will come to an end. If we are patient and steadfast in faith, suffering will bring us endless happiness, as Jesus promised, 'Blessed are you that weep now, for you shall laugh' (Luke 6:21). In heaven we will rejoice at His side for ever and ever.

Heaven is stronger than hell, overcoming torture and transforming the diabolical conditions of prisons and labour camps. Let us live now in the reality of the world above and all that awaits us there, and even when we are in the depths of suffering, persecution and torment, we will not lose this source of never-ending joy.

Heaven's everlasting splendour
Paint for us in glowing colours,
Lord of heaven, King of joy.
As we drink in heaven's glory,
Feast our souls upon its beauty,
All our trials will fade away.

Oh, may earthly woes and suffering
Never blind us to the glory
Which awaits us evermore.
Let us trust when faced with horrors:
Heaven's ours amid the terrors.
Suffering will then lose its pain.

Heaven, where our home's for ever,
Heaven with its drawing power,
Lifting out of pain and grief,
You refresh my soul in suffering,
Fear and weeping overcoming.
None can rob me of your joy.

Chapter 7

Strong in the Lord

Watch and pray. Matthew 26:41

JESUS, IN HIS GREAT LOVE for His disciples, sought to prepare them for the coming time of testing. In three predictions of His sufferings He indicated that the hour of His crucifixion was approaching. We know how the disciples reacted. It was as if they had not heard what their Lord and Master had said. Do we today hear His words about the end-time sufferings, which will entail a worldwide persecution of Christians (see, for instance, Matthew 24:9; John 15:20)? Do we see the signs of 'creeping persecution' in Western society?

If only we would realize how imminent the hour of trial is and not shut our eyes to the facts! Non-believers, the people of this world, are wiser than believers, as Jesus observes (see Luke 16:8). They are quick to grasp the implications of the world situation. Jesus' warning not to act like the people in Noah's time is addressed primarily to us Christians: 'They were eating and drinking, marrying and giving in marriage' when destruction overtook them (Matthew 24:37–39).

Jesus wants to help us before it is too late. This He

can do only if we realistically face up to the threat of a widespread persecution of Christians and a major world disaster.

'Watch and pray!' said Jesus to His disciples in Gethsemane, and the Bible tells us that Jesus Himself 'prayed more earnestly' (Luke 22:44). In the hour of affliction only those will be strong who pray much now, following the admonition of Holy Scripture: 'First of all, then, I urge that supplications, prayers ... be made' (1 Timothy 2:1). Prayer should now be our first priority. The best part of our time should go to prayer—even at the expense of sleep, personal interests and hobbies.

Our commitment to endure suffering is something we can bring to God only in our prayers, for only in prayer can we completely surrender our will to Him in the assurance that He will not let us be tempted beyond our strength. Such an act of commitment can also be written down—if the Spirit so leads us—for praying again and again. If we have struggled through to the point where we can say, 'Your will be done', our hearts will be immersed in peace. Dedication to the will of God, as He leads us into the time of persecution, will make us strong in the hour of trial.

Inseparably linked with the prayer of dedication is a trusting spirit, for what we experience will be according to our faith. And in whom are we placing our trust?—The almighty God who made heaven and earth. Our help will come most assuredly from Him, even in the hardest moments. We believe in Jesus, the mighty Victor and Helper, to whom the wind and waves, yes, all things are subject. If it is difficult for us to pray, then we may find it helpful to repeat a verse like this as a starter:

I believe and will not waver.
I will trust in You, my Father,
For You always send me help.

By affirming our faith, we will make it grow. With our trust strengthened through prayer, we will be able to endure the ordeals of persecution and have the courage to confess our allegiance to Jesus. We will continue to witness to Him regardless of the consequences and be faithful to Him to the very end.

Today God is waiting for our prayer of faith. He has promised to answer prayer, and His name is Yes and Amen. In our prayer times today we receive what we need for tomorrow—a trusting spirit and the courage to endure suffering and to stand up for our faith.

Acceptance of suffering and the prayer of faith go hand in hand with the struggle against sin. Those who now resist their sins with the utmost determination as they battle in faith and prayer will be strong in the hour of trial, for then their sins will not cling to them. Sin entangles and weakens us. It makes us fail and despair in times of testing. We may even be capable of denying Jesus, betraying our fellow Christians and falling away from God. However, those who now fight out every issue in prayer and overcome by the blood of the Lamb will then be strong in the Lord.

Chapter 8

The Hour of Gethsemane for the World

They went to a place which was called Gethsemane; and he said to his disciples...'My soul is very sorrowful, even to death; remain here, and watch.' Mark 14:32–34

IN GETHSEMANE JESUS WAS FACED with the destruction of His work and the end of His life. He wrestled with death, the powerful prince of darkness, who tormented Him with the utmost cruelty.

What was the significance of Gethsemane? In this decisive battle God the Father accomplished His wonderful purpose in Jesus, evoking from Him a special prayer which strengthened Him for the approaching horrors and the ordeal of the crucifixion when He would bear God's punishment for us. It was a prayer in which Jesus expressed complete acceptance of the Father's will. Prayer was Jesus' weapon in this hour of darkness. The Gospels record that Jesus 'knelt down and prayed.'—'Again, for the second time, he went away and prayed.'—'And being in an agony he prayed more earnestly; and his sweat became like great drops of blood falling down upon the ground' (Luke 22:41,44; Matthew 26:42).

Now to apply this event to our lives: In the present hour of darkness, with demons surrounding and attacking us, we, too, are challenged to pray. Jesus asks us now, as He asked His disciples long ago, 'Why do you sleep? Rise and pray that you may not enter into temptation' (Luke 22:46).

First of all, we need to pray for ourselves, since we are exposed to unprecedented attacks by the powers of darkness. The danger of being sucked into deception and lawlessness is very real. The atmosphere is oppressive, generating fear and depression. Demonic powers are trying to draw us into defeatism, and we are tempted to yield, especially when we see members of our family falling prey to the enemy. We feel weak and powerless in the face of the ever-advancing forces of evil. We can expect no help from people. But then Jesus' mighty call reaches our ears: Pray!

The Letter of James expounds on this: 'Resist the devil and he will flee from you. Draw near to God and he will draw near to you' (chapter 4:7–8). Prayer means drawing near to God, coming into contact with Him and bringing Him all our problems, everything that depresses us. Then the situation will be changed. God deals with our troubles when we bring them to Him in prayer. He takes action. He transforms the depression, discouragement and despair in our hearts, filling us instead with peace, strength, comfort and deep joy. Through prayer we discover what a kind and loving Father we have in God. In these terrible times He holds us, His children, close to His heart. He strengthens us and by His Spirit imparts to us the courage to suffer. Prayer is not an art acquired only by mature Christians. We can start praying from the moment we have come to know the Lord.

Prayer means calling upon the name of Jesus, the Prince of Victory, the Lamb of God. As the sacrificial Lamb, He overcame Satan at Calvary, destroying his power. Whenever we call upon Jesus, our Champion, in these satanic times, the demons seeking to oppress us are put to flight. They are trying to fill our hearts with despair and unbelief, and rob us of all power, joy and assurance of victory. Therefore, we are challenged, as never before, to pray and engage in spiritual warfare.

Jesus is Victor! Jesus is Victor!

We cannot pray these words often enough. They have power whether we pray them silently or aloud. Then the forces of darkness that sought to ensnare us will yield. This prayer is our refuge in an age rife with deception, false teachings, diabolic influences and satanic cults. If we do as Jesus says, praying in this worldwide hour of Gethsemane and proclaiming Him Victor, we will overcome and be comforted and strengthened. We will experience His help in every battle and hardship. When we turn our eyes upon Jesus in prayer, we behold the mighty Prince of Victory, who conquered hell and Satan. Then amid the hardships and distress of the present age, triumphant joy will take hold of our hearts: Jesus is victorious—He will come again as Lord and King.

But even today He is with us as our Lord and Helper. Prayer alone gave Jesus, the Son of God, the strength to endure the dark hour of Gethsemane. How can we as sinners expect to receive the strength to endure our Gethsemanes other than by prayer?

When Jesus prayed in Gethsemane, He prayed a

very special prayer, a prayer of tremendous power that drove away Satan, a prayer expressive of deepest adoration. Jesus prayed, 'My Father...not as I will, but as thou wilt' (Matthew 26:39). The prayer 'Yes, Father' cost Jesus the deepest agony of soul. It was an unconditional surrender to the greatest suffering of all. Paintings by famous masters show Jesus prostrate on the ground as He prayed, 'Thy will be done!' For the Son of God, who possesses all might, it was an act of complete surrender: I commit Myself to Your will, even though I do not understand it. I trust in You and in Your leadings, even if it means facing the ruin of My life-work, even if it means that My disciples will forsake Me. I surrender Myself even if it means that death and the powers of hell kill Me now. Here I am. I am Yours to do with as You please.

The dark hour of Gethsemane has arrived for the world and now Jesus is challenging us to pray as He did. Peace will enter our hearts only if we follow His example, for then our will abides in the will of God. We may wish to express our dedication to Him with the following prayer: 'Yes, Father, Your ways are perfect. I accept them even if it means living in these terrible times. I give You my consent. You have planned everything in my life, and Your will is good. I know that You are leading me to the eternal goal. You are my prize and reward, and in heaven I will behold You and suffering will be banished for evermore!'

> God is guiding ever onward
> To an awe-inspiring goal,
> Heaven's everlasting glory,
> Peace and joy for evermore.

God's ways often pass through darkness
On to glory for all those
Who immerse their wills in His will
As contented, child-like souls.

All God's leadings for His children
Testify of love divine.
And along the darkest pathways
His love all the more will shine.

'Your ways are perfect'—'Your judgments are true and just!' Short prayers like these will help us to surrender our will ever anew and to bear the afflictions of the present era. Through such an act of dedication suffering loses its hold on us. Without a life of intensive prayer, we will be lost in this demonic age, overwhelmed by our trials and temptations and by all that is frightening, sad and depressing. If we want to experience help and deliverance in time of persecution and disaster, we need to lead a life of prayer, forming a deep relationship of love with Jesus and the Father. Prayer changes everything. But who is it who prays much?—Only those who regard themselves as weak and sinful, for they turn to Jesus, sensing their great need of Him. And Jesus has promised to come to the poor in spirit, the penitent sinners. He will enter their hearts and live there.

Chapter 9

Approaching the Time of Testing

May the Lord direct your hearts to the love of God and to the steadfastness of Christ. 2 Thessalonians 3:5

WHEN PERSECUTION COMES upon us, it is essential that Jesus Christ lives in us as our great love. If I love someone, I can suffer for him. Through a life of prayer we give Jesus more and more room within us. Whatever fills our hearts in the time of distress will dominate us. If it is Jesus, then He—and not the adversity and misery—will have power over us. But if earthly things, our family, career, prestige, well-being, personal security and self engross us, then we will not have the strength to endure affliction. Only in Jesus Christ do we find the strength that enables us to overcome in suffering. It is imperative that He lives in us.

Of the believers sent to prison or labour camp for Jesus' sake, those whose hearts were filled with many earthly things proved to be weak. They found it hard to bear any loss. Their hearts craved for everything that they no longer had and they fell into despair when forced to live under distressing conditions. Thus Jesus was unable to break through with His comfort, peace and joy.

In contrast, believers whose hearts were filled with Jesus and free from slavery to earthly things and desires were able to endure cross-examination and various forms of torture, for Jesus lived in them and no one could rob them of Him. Jesus was their first and foremost love. And this 'first' love, this exclusive love for Jesus, gives a person the strength to suffer.

Those who are aflame with love for Jesus will experience the truth of His promise: 'If a man loves me, he will keep my word, and my Father will love him, and we will come to him and make our home with him' (John 14:23). If our Lord and Saviour lives in our hearts, this means we are indwelt by the One who has all power in heaven and on earth, and we are strong in Him. It means we are indwelt by the One who is eternal love, and in His love we are secure and all our fears are expelled. He is the One whose power is manifested in our weakness (2 Corinthians 12:9), enabling us to overcome and persevere. Not even the greatest sufferings can drown the joy He gives us, for He is everlasting joy. As the crown of heaven, He makes heaven's glory and joy come down when we are in deep suffering.

So let us pray for this first love, this ardent, bridal love for Jesus. Then we will experience during persecution the truth of the scripture: 'Love is strong as death...Its flashes are flashes of fire, a most vehement flame. Many waters cannot quench love, neither can floods drown it' (Song of Solomon 8:6–7).

Chapter 10

Training Starts Now

1. Let us prepare ourselves by reading the Word of God daily and storing it not just in our memories but in our hearts. Let us cultivate a deep love for the Word of God now, applying it to our lives, so that during suffering and persecution—even if our Bible is taken away from us—it will be a source of strength to us, and our relationship to God in Jesus will be reinforced.

2. Every time difficulties and impossible situations arise in our daily life, let us believe in the omnipotence of God and His fatherly aid. Let us not yield to worry, but trust completely in the Father's tender, loving care: He never gives us more than we can bear and always has ways and means to help. Then by the time persecution breaks out, we will be 'practised in faith' so that we can experience His aid.

3. Let us bear small bodily ailments—pain, weakness and fatigue—with faith in the power of Jesus' blood, which sustains us and renews our strength. Then we will be prepared for the future when the physical suffering will be far greater.

4. When faced with difficulties and bewildering situations, let us surrender our will; and when chastened, let us humble ourselves beneath the mighty hand of God. May our response always be: 'Yes, Father, Your judgments are just, both now and in the future.'

5. Let us keep looking to Jesus, so that we may have the right perspective. Seeing in spirit the Man of Sorrows, acquainted with grief, will enable us to suffer. Focusing on the mighty Victor over sin and Satan will strengthen us.

6. Let us claim in faith Jesus' redemption in our daily battle against our judgmental attitudes, pride, stinginess, envy, self-will, egoism, anger, the desires of the flesh, and bondage to people and things. Then sin will not be able to weaken us in the future and, if we are sent to prison or labour camp, we can be a witness to those around us by radiating the love and peace of Jesus.

7. Let us endure every hardship, great or small, for love of Jesus, so that when we have to undergo pain and torment in persecution, our spontaneous reaction will be, 'I will bear it for Your sake, Jesus.'

8. Let us live in close fellowship with Jesus now, conversing with Him at all times and doing everything for Him in love, so that love, which is the strongest power of all, will give us the strength to undergo suffering in the time of persecution.

9. Let us lead a life of prayer now, so that prayer will

be our constant resort in trials and temptations, in times of loneliness, anguish and suffering. When we pray, Jesus draws near to us, bringing us heaven on earth.

10. Let us fight resolutely against the desire for popularity and prestige or the fear of giving offence, so that we can overcome cowardice. Let us commit ourselves to making an uncompromising stand for the Lord, seeking His approval in everything. Then during persecution we will be willing to pay the price of our convictions.

11. Let us do good now to those who hurt us and treat us unjustly. Let us bless them and show them love in thought, word and deed. Then later we will have the right attitude towards our persecutors. Instead of judging them, we will be able to encounter them like a lamb with meekness and compassion, in the humble awareness of our own sin.

12. Every time we are at a loss as to what to say in some situation or conversation, let us trust the Holy Spirit implicitly to guide us and give us His words, now and also at future trials and cross-examinations.

13. Today let us count on Jesus making heaven a reality in our lives. Let us be heavenly-minded, so that during persecution we can rejoice in the assurance, 'Suffering will come to an end, and everlasting glory will follow.'

PRAYERS

Dedication of the Will

My Father,

During this time of preparation
help me to practise submitting my will to Yours,
dedicating myself to it,
so that in the time of affliction
I can completely rest in Your will.

I believe that Your will is pure goodness
and that all the paths You lead me on,
including paths of suffering
in the time of persecution,
are according to Your plan of love.
The final outcome will not be suffering
but great joy at Your throne
for all eternity.

My Father,

I worship You for everything
You have ordained for my life
and for the lives of my dear ones,
even if Your leadings seem hard now

and however bitter they may be
in the coming times.
Take my will and my life.
Do with me as You please,
whether Your will brings me
joy or suffering, life or death.

I surrender myself unreservedly to You
in the implicit faith
that everything You do is good—
not only for me but for my dear ones as well.
You always have our best interests at heart.

Amen.

Trusting in the Love of God

My Father,

Even before the foundation of the world
You ordained what will happen to me
every day, every hour, during persecution.
You know me.
You know my character, my powers of endurance.
You know whether I am weak or strong,
and before sending anything into my life,
You first weigh it.

Your loving heart ensures
that I will not be tempted beyond my strength
in the trials and testings during persecution.
Of that I can be certain.
My Father, if anyone has evil intentions for me,
You only have to speak a word
and his attempts will be foiled.
My torturers can never do more to me
than You permit.
And Jesus will give me the strength to endure.

Lord Jesus, take my life.
I am willing to suffer and even die for You
out of love and gratitude,
for You have loved me and brought me salvation
through Your agonizing death on the cross.

Amen.

Prayer for 'First Love'

My Lord Jesus,

The day is coming when I may have to tread a path that You have trodden before me—a path where I am exposed to hatred, subjected to imprisonment, trials, beatings, physical and mental torture. And so I have a special request, which I bring daily before You in this time of preparation:

Give me the first love, that ardent love for You, Lord Jesus, which will be greater than the suffering.

My Lord Jesus,

I need the love for You that the Early Christians had. Otherwise I will not be able to endure the coming sufferings—sufferings such as the world has never seen before. Give me this love, I pray, which is stronger than any hardship, even stronger than death. Give me this love, which no fire can consume, so that I will not deny You under the pressure of persecution, but remain faithful to You to the end.

Above all, give me repentance for all the times when my love for You was lukewarm and half-hearted and when I did not love You first and foremost, with all my strength and with full devotion, as You have bidden us. Give me the brokenness of heart out of which love for You is born.

I renounce every false tie, everything hindering, loosening or severing my relationship of love with You: enslavement to self, a false attachment to my family or a particular person, bondage to my job, to prestige or possessions. I renounce every lifestyle and behaviour pattern contrary to God's commandments and grievous and dishonouring to You. Give me the determination to break with all this and to claim Your redemption, so that love for You will have room in my heart. From now on I want to live for You instead of for myself, my wishes and desires. From now on I am willing to suffer for You.

My Lord Jesus, O Lamb of God, fill my heart with love for You, so that I will follow You into affliction and death as Your little lamb, suffering out of love and in thanksgiving for Your agonizing suffering and bitter death. I believe You will give me this strong and ardent love by the power of Your blood.

Amen.

❧

I Love You, Lord

I love You, Lord, the loveliest and fairest,
And all I am and have is Yours, dear Jesus.
Within my heart You dwell and have Your throne,
O Lamb of God and Bridegroom of my soul,
 Beloved Lamb.

I love You, Lord; You gave Your life to save me,
And now my life, my all, are Yours completely.
I love You, Lord, and yearn to be Your own,
Your very own, dear Lord, all Yours alone,
 All Yours alone.

I love You, Lord, oh, hear my song of ardour,
My song of love's devotion and deep fervour.
King of my heart, beloved God and Lord,
Your bride is Yours now and for evermore,
 For ever Yours.

And soon I'll see You face to face, dear Saviour,
Awesome in majesty and peerless splendour.
Then from my heart a stream of love will flow
In worship, praise, thanksgiving, wondering awe
 Unceasingly.

Prayer for the Time of Testing

Lord Jesus,

Be my sole possession today in joy and suffering, so that in the time of testing You will be my deepest consolation and foremost love, inspiring me to follow You wherever You go.

Grant that I may never leave You. Let me always choose You and never the easy way out, even in hardship and adversity.

In the hour of trial let this love be alive in my heart, so that I may comfort You, glorify Your name and make it known to many.

I believe that in Your love You will never abandon me and that in my hour of greatest need my prayers will be answered. Your faithfulness is my shield and refuge.

Amen.
Mother Martyria

Prayer for Faithfulness

Jesus,
You make me strong, courageous
and steadfast,
all afire with love for You,
wholly dedicated and firm,
unyielding as rock with one single aim:
I want Jesus, only Jesus!
I am ready to suffer for You.
I will not seek relief or ease,
nor try to understand You.
All I want, dear Lord,
is by faith to embrace You
and to love You even in the night
of trials and suffering.

Amen.
Mother Martyria

Prayer of Readiness

My Lord Jesus,
I believe that the immeasurable
greatness of the power of God,
which He manifested in You
when He raised You from the dead,
will also be effective in me
when I am weak in body, soul or spirit.

Lord Jesus, I cannot expect anything of myself,
but I look to You for everything.
You will not fail me.
You are close by me, ever ready to help.

Lord Jesus, give me what I lack:
fearlessness and courage to witness,
strength to suffer and an ardent love.
I believe in Your promise and am counting on it.

Lord Jesus, help me to fix my eyes
on the goal above.
Soon the suffering will be over
and transformed into glory at Your side
for all eternity.

For love of You, Lord Jesus,
and in thanksgiving for Your redemption
I offer You my life.
May it bring You joy and comfort.

Here I am, my Lord Jesus.
I am ready to enter suffering for You,
trusting in the power of Your blood shed for me.

Amen.

Jesus, My Love Is Yours

Jesus, my love is Yours;
Jesus, my life is Yours,
Jesus, my joy and my crown.
Sun of my life You are.
I'm but a little star
Shining for You in the night.

Jesus, I'll go with You,
My crown and precious jewel,
When darkness covers my path.
You are my heart's delight
Even in darkest night.
I will remain at Your side.

Keep me, Lord, close to You.
Oh, make me one with You,
Dwelling within Your own heart.
I have but one desire:
Ever in You to abide
Till I see You face to face.

Grace to Bear Our Cross

Lord Jesus,
When I think of Your great suffering
as You bore the cross to Calvary
and endured the crucifixion,
I believe that You have won the victory
over my reluctance to bear my cross.
I believe that You will give me
the dedication to endure the coming affliction.

Out of thanksgiving and love for You,
who bore the cross for me to Calvary
in immeasurable pain,
I will say from now on:

I want my cross.
It comes from Your hands,
and so I will accept it.
Lay the cross on me.

I want my cross,
from which streams of blessing flow.
It is laden with gold.
And it is never too heavy,
for it comes from Your loving heart

and You have weighed it first
to see whether I can bear it.

I want my cross,
which transforms me into Your image.
It is precious and dear to me.
It helps prepare me
to inherit the heavenly glory.

I want my cross.
I want to carry it and follow You,
O Cross-Bearer, Lord Jesus.
I will accompany You on Your path
and trust that in the face of Your sufferings
my own will grow small and insignificant.

When in pain and suffering,
I want to thank You for counting me worthy
to bear the cross and suffering for Your sake,
Lord Jesus Christ.
I want to suffer for You,
who died to save me.
I owe You my life, my all.

I want to thank You
for the privilege of entering
into the fellowship of Your sufferings
and of living in expectation of the resurrection,
the heavenly glory.

Help me to do as Your Word says,
'Rejoice in so far as you share
Christ's sufferings.'
One day above I will rejoice at Your side
for all eternity.

Amen.

May This Day Be Dedicated

May this day be dedicated
To You, Jesus, dearest Lord.
Troubles, cares—whatever it brings me,
May Your name be praised, adored.

Lamb of God, beloved Bridegroom,
Grant Your grace to me this day,
That I may reflect Your image
In all that I do and say.

Help me to endure each trial,
Dearest Jesus, hear my plea.
Even on the hardest pathway
May You, Lord, be seen in me.

May I live to bring You glory
When Your name is so despised,
In all things, whatever may happen,
Prove myself Your faithful bride.

Prayer for the Right Kind of Fear

Lord Jesus,

Put the right kind of fear into my heart. Grant that I may no longer fear suffering, for You say, 'Fear not! I am with you.' But You also say, 'Fear him who can destroy both soul and body in hell.'

So take away my wrong kind of fear and fill me instead with a loving confidence in You and Your help, which You have firmly promised me and which will therefore never fail me.

Let me fear sin, which delivers me into Satan's hands and can bring me the sufferings of hell in eternity.

Prepare me now by giving me light about my sins, so that I can confess them before it is too late, obtain forgiveness through Your precious blood and turn from my old ways in repentance, thus making Satan lose his claim on me.

Let me grieve over my sins, and give me a humble, contrite heart, so that I may partake of Your grace, upon which I am totally dependent in the time of affliction, and can enter the heavenly glory afterwards.

I believe that You will help me to overcome sin and fear by the power of Your redemption, which is imparted to penitent sinners. Grant that in the midst of hardship and disgrace, affliction and death, I may glorify You with my life.

Amen.

Gethsemane Prayer

Lord Jesus,

I pray, make me Your little lamb by the time persecution begins, dedicated to God's will and humbly following You, however and wherever You lead me, even if it means prison, labour camp or death.

I want to go with You, O Lamb of God, my Lord and Saviour, who wore chains for my sake. In everyday life I want to keep looking to You, remembering how You quietly and humbly allowed the guards to bind and arrest You, O Ruler of the world. And as I do so, prepare me, so that I might be a testimony before the visible and invisible world.

Help me to practise now by willingly enduring all that is hard for me, so that I may enter an ever deeper union with You. When my hour comes, Lord Jesus, give me the strength to say, 'Here I am!' and let me radiate Your humility, love and peace. And having bound myself to You, let me be faithful to You unto death—to Your glory.

Amen.

Prayer of Trust

My Lord Jesus,
I thank You for the assurance
that You will manifest Yourself to me
in my plight
as the One who subdues
the wind and waves of destruction.

Even now I give praise
that no matter how great
the forces of terror and destruction are,
Your power to help is greater still,
for Your might and strength are unequalled.

I firmly believe that if my fear
on the day of terror is great
and threatens to consume me,
Your peace and comfort, which surround me,
will be even greater.

In the face of destruction
I will keep my eyes on You,
for You are coming to demonstrate
Your power and help,
and to manifest Your love to me.

I believe that the overwhelming sense
of Your presence will change everything,
transforming hell into heaven
in the time of distress.

I trust in Your heavenly hosts
and their aid.
I believe that You send Your angels
to minister to those who are to obtain salvation,
and especially to those undergoing
affliction and persecution.

O Holy Spirit,
I believe that as my Counsellor
You will give me guidance
in the coming time of chaos and confusion
when no one else can advise me.
I firmly believe You will prompt me
to make the right decisions
and help me to make the right moves.

Loving Father,
I thank You for the comforting assurance
that with Your almighty hand covering me
I will suffer no harm
in the time of persecution.

I trust in Your love.
You will care for me
in every frightening experience,
for You are my Father.
When the way grows dark,
You will take me, Your child,
by the hand and bring me through.

Amen.

When the Waves Rise Ever Higher

When the waves rise ever higher
I will sing that my Deliverer
Is aboard my storm-tossed boat.
He commands, 'Begone, all terror!
As the Lord over wind and weather,
I will cover you, My child.'

At the height of our affliction,
Overwhelmed by apprehension,
We are strengthened by the Lord.
'Fear not,' He declares. 'I'm coming,
Trouble, fear, distress rebuking.
At My word the waves are calm.

I am there, your God and Saviour,
Shielding you with loving fervour
And dispelling every fear,
My own peace to you imparting,
Till your heart in Mine is resting.
Peace is yours if you believe.'

Faith for Now and Later

Lord Jesus,
I believe You are with me, helping me.
And in the time of great affliction
You will strengthen me.

In my suffering
I immerse myself in Your suffering
and my will in Yours, which is pure goodness.
And in all my fear and agony
I take refuge in Your wounds.

As I turn my eyes upon You, Lord Jesus,
I am comforted.
O Man of Sorrows, my heart clings to You.
You are with me,
and when You touch my soul,
I am strengthened.

Lord Jesus, I trust in You.
You are my shield
and Your angels are watching over me.
And I know that my Father is carrying me through.

Lord Jesus, I thank You.
Heaven beckons and the crown shines brightly.
Soon my suffering will be over.
And so I will persevere,
for Your blood is my strength;
it makes the weak strong.

Lord Jesus, I am suffering with You and for You,
and that brings glory.

Amen.

Petitions for the Hour of Trial

Lord Jesus Christ, I come to You
in the assurance that You answer prayer,
as You promised.

Give me the strength to suffer
and persevere to the end.
Help me to believe that You will be with me,
giving me a foretaste of heaven.

Grant that in my distress I may see You
as the Man of Sorrows in Your suffering—
and let this be a source of strength for me.

Give me the faith
that Your help will never fail me
but will come in my plight.

Let me cling to the assurance
that nothing can separate me from You.

Let Your peace fill my heart,
and Your love enfold me.

Grant that I may now love You
with a strong and tender love,
so that this love will give me
the strength to suffer and even die for You.

Give me the courage to witness,
and set me free from all fear of others.

Help me both now and later
in the time of great affliction
to say 'Yes, Father' ever anew.

Give me the grace to lose my life
for love of You.
Help me to make the small sacrifices
of everyday life
and the far greater sacrifices
that will later be required of me.

Grant that I may be a witness for You
in the acute sufferings
that the time of persecution will bring.

Help me to rejoice amid fear and distress
at the thought that soon I will be
with You for ever in the heavenly glory.

Amen.

Prayer of Thanks

Loving Father,

Thank You for the assurance that in the time of distress You will manifest Yourself as a true father. I trust You and believe that while we sow tears in the vale of sorrows and persecution You will refresh us and then let us reap joy eternally in heaven. You always let the sun shine upon Your children after the rain and give them laughter after their tears. You comfort and cheer them with Your love and in heaven above endow them with glory for ever.

Praise be to Your fatherly heart, full of tender love for us! You create tremendous glory and joy out of suffering if we bear it patiently with a trusting heart, steadfastness and humility—for love of You.

Loving Father, in times of utmost darkness and agony I want to remember that what we suffer at this present time will come to an end and that You have prepared for us a life of glory in Your city above.

Thank You that everything on this earth is transient—even the hardest moments and periods—whereas the good seeds sown then will grow and bring forth fruit, which I will reap with joy in eternity.

I thank You that in Your love You have so ordained it that earthly suffering is short-lived, whereas the glory of heaven will last for ever and ever.

Amen.

Faithful to the End

Jesus, my Lord and Saviour,
when You are so blasphemed and degraded today,
I want to pledge myself in love
to stand up and be counted for You,
no matter what it may cost me
in the way of sacrifices and suffering
both now and during persecution.

You will give me the strength not to heed
shame and humiliation for Your sake.
And when I am ridiculed, isolated or attacked
for professing You as my Lord and Saviour,
You will enable me to bear this in love for You
and without feelings of resentment.

Let my love for You grow more and more ardent
so that I will be able to undergo
the greatest affliction, even martyrdom.
Keep me faithful to the very end.

Amen.

Prayer for the Persecuted

Leader:
Lord, You said: 'Call upon me in the day of trouble; I will deliver you.' We call upon You for...(insert accordingly).

All:
Deliver them from their distress; loosen their chains; send them Your angels.

Leader:
Lord, You said: 'The Holy Spirit will teach you in that very hour what you ought to say.'

All:
We trust You and believe that You will keep Your promise and put Your words into their mouths.

Leader:
Lord, You said, 'Fear not, for I am with you.'

All:
We pray that the sense of Your presence will make hardships easy for them to bear, and the bitter sweet.

Leader:
Lord, You said, 'Blessed are you when men revile you and persecute you...on my account...Rejoice in that day, and leap for joy.'

All:
Give them joy in their hearts at the privilege of suffering for You.

Leader:
Lord, You said: 'You shall be my witnesses.'

All:
Give them strength to be real witnesses to You before their oppressors, so that they can help win many souls for You.

Leader:
Lord, You said: 'As one whom his mother comforts, so I will comfort you.'

All:
Let these words come true for them in the darkest hours of distress and inner conflict.

Leader:
Lord, You said: 'Your Father knows what you need.'

All:
Our Father, we believe that You will care for their physical needs as their Father and satisfy their souls with Your presence.

Amen.

In all these things
we are more than conquerors
through him who loved us.
For I am sure that neither death, nor life,
nor angels, nor principalities,
nor things present, nor things to come,
nor powers, nor height, nor depth,
nor anything else in all creation,
will be able to separate us
from the love of God in Christ Jesus our Lord.

Romans 8:37–39

Other literature by M. Basilea Schlink

YOURS IS THE VICTORY AND MAJESTY 96 pages

Readers comment: A stirring, dynamic piece of literature. * The insight it gives about future events is something every Christian should know. * How wonderfully the Spirit explains everything to God's children! * The best analysis of the present situation I've come across. Profound, discerning. * Superb orientation for our times.

REPENTANCE—THE JOY-FILLED LIFE 96 pages

'This book unfolds God's answer to one of the greatest needs in the churches of our time. If you are looking for new life, joy and power for your own spiritual life and for those around you, then this book is a must.'

THE HIDDEN TREASURE IN SUFFERING 96 pages

Cares — Strained Relationships — Fear — Illness — Weariness — Loneliness — Inner Conflict — Personality Problems — Unanswered Prayers — Untalented — Growing Old — Want and Need — Fear of Death — Unfair Treatment — Facing Hatred and Slander... From the wealth of her personal experience Mother Basilea shares how we can find the treasure that lies hidden in every trial and hardship.

DOES OUR WORLD HAVE A FUTURE? 48 pages

If only we knew what to expect in the future! Some kind of clarity would help overcome the paralyzing effect of the current world instability—especially if it is a view that awakens hope. Mother Basilea once again directs our attention to the Bible and opens up for us an unusual perspective of the future.

ESCAPING THE WEB OF DECEPTION 64 pages

At a time when Christian values are being questioned or compromised, spiritual discernment is of utmost importance to those who love Jesus and want to follow Him. This book helps give insight into today's trends.

NEW AGE—FROM A BIBLICAL VIEWPOINT
32 pages

'Your book is outstanding and contains vital information. I would like to pass it on above all to parents and young people, seeing that occult groups are mushrooming everywhere.'

SONGS FOR SPIRITUAL WARFARE 48 pages

Here we are offered spiritual armament for overthrowing satanic strongholds, freeing captives, cancelling curses and experiencing release from demonic bondage and oppression. In an age when the power of evil and curses are a greater reality than ever, we need to know how to turn Satan's attacks to our advantage.

PRAYING OUR WAY THROUGH LIFE 48 pages

'...came just at the right moment in my life. I was asking questions of Him: "Why again?" This booklet answered my questions and I praised Him for His timing.'

BRIDE OF JESUS CHRIST 64 pages

No unattainable goal is described here, but the ultimate which the love of God has planned for us. All those who long to draw nearer to Him will find an answer to their quest in these pages.

THE UNSEEN WORLD OF ANGELS AND DEMONS
144 pages

We need to know our enemy if we are to defeat him. But we also need to know the weapons God has provided for us. After describing the origin of evil and providing evidence of demonic activity, the author focuses on the victory that is ours in Jesus Christ and the role of angels in the world today. For to assist us in the combat with the evil one, God has sent us the armies of heaven—His angels.